COSMO's
500
SECRETS
ABOUT
MEN

COSMO's
500
SECRETS
ABOUT
MEN

From the Editors of **COSMOPOLITAN**

51
Find out how
often he dreams
about sex

61
The real reason
he feels those
butterflies
around you

CONTENTS

123
The time of day he's extra horny

226
The reason he eats like an animal

207

Don't keep him waiting in bed. Find out why.

Preface

Each month, millions of women rely on Cosmo for candid, useful insight into men. And now we've put together tons of that famous knowhow into one convenient little package: *500 Secrets About Men*. It's full of fascinating, random, and sometimes hilarious facts about guys that you'll want to read, learn from, and share with your friends. Want to know the odds that he'll call you after a first date? Or the most sensitive part of his body during foreplay? It's all right here.

This book was designed to give you quick hits of fun and revealing info that you can flip through whenever, wherever. Start from the beginning or jump to the section that interests you most. By the time you get to the 500th secret, you'll have learned exactly what makes your guy tick (or any man, for that matter).

So are you ready to get a totally uncensored guide to the opposite sex? Just turn the page (although we think secret number 253 is so juicy, you might want to read it first).

—From the Editors of Cosmo

THE BASICS

To understand what makes guys tick, you have to start with the fundamentals. That's why we're kicking off this man book with some juicy facts about his most primal attributes— his brain, his body, and even what his sleep positions reveal about him. We know you'll be fascinated by the tidbits we dug up here. Especially fact number 39. You'll know why when you get there....

Mirror neurons—the parts of the brain that let you pick up on another person's gesture, body posture, and facial expressions—are smaller in men than they are in women. That's why women are good at empathizing with others while guys generally aren't.

His Brain

2 Stressful interactions trigger the fight-or-flight area of his brain (whereas in women, they activate the area responsible for nurturing).

3 Men have a smaller anterior cingulate cortex (aka the worrywart center of the brain) than women do. That's why your guy may tend to be less anxious than you.

4 The sense of smell travels a direct route to the limbic lobe of the brain, where it can trigger an emotional reaction. This is why biologists believe that a woman's scent can so instantly turn a man on (and vice versa).

5

In a man's brain, the bridge that communicates between the two hemispheres is smaller than in a woman's, so it can't handle as much thought traffic—which explains why dudes are more single-minded and have a harder time multitasking.

6 When guys look at an angry face (e.g., your expression after finding out he deleted your favorite show from the DVR), their brains show less activity in the area that interprets emotion, which explains why your guy has a hard time understanding where you're coming from.

Surprisingly, a guy's feet—and especially his toes—have a neurological connection to his penis. The area of his brain that regulates foot sensation is situated right next to the region that controls his erection.

HERS

HIS

8

The sexual-pursuit area of a guy's brain is about two and a half times bigger than a woman's.

9 When a guy finds a woman attractive, the visual centers of his brain light up and the cognitive centers slow down. As a result, his mind becomes focused on what he's seeing rather than allowing him to think clearly.

10 The planum temporale, a portion of the brain that recognizes and uses language cues, is thinner in men than it is in women—which is why guys often don't pick up on what you mean when you say subtle things.

The spot in his brain that registers love is very close to the area that processes pain. Since they share a location, he'll actually stop hurting if he thinks of you.

12 Men have a smaller insula (the part of the brain that's in charge of gut feelings), which makes them less intuitive than women.

13 Guys perceive beauty using the right side of their brain, which registers the big picture as opposed to tiny details. That explains why men pick up on the overall effect ("she's hot") and not the small stuff (like a chipped nail).

In the part of the brain that's linked to the desire for food, men show less activity than women do. This ability to switch off hunger thoughts may help explain lower rates of obesity in guys.

If a guy is ripped, he has more testosterone, which means he is more likely to be fertile.

His Body

16 When a woman's voice is modulated and energetic, with highs and lows, it can increase a dude's heart rate and boost the amount of testosterone in his blood.

17 The reason men always keep the TV volume so loud? They can't hear as well as women can.

18 Tall men report higher levels of life satisfaction.

19

A man's skin is 10 times less sensitive than a woman's...

HERS   HIS

20 ...and his sense of smell is about 20 percent less keen than yours too.

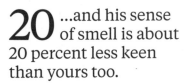

21 When a man is aroused, his perspiration becomes saturated with chemicals that are more appealing to the opposite sex.

22 His body is strongest midmorning, when he has the most cortisol and adrenaline pumping (the hormones that give him energy).

23 There's no scientific link between the size of his feet and the size of his package.

24

The more intelligent a man is, the better his sperm quality. One study found that guys who scored well on verbal and math tests had more swimmers with better motility.

25 Men have more heat-generating muscle mass than women, which explains why you can be in the same room as a guy and freezing your butt off, yet he's totally fine.

26 In fact, the ideal room temp for a normal-size man in his 20s is about 6 degrees colder than for a woman.

27 Men are bad at ID-ing colors because their retinas contain fewer cells that pick up on hues.

28 Research shows that the scent of a woman's tears causes a man's libido to drop.

29 His lips have the thinnest layer of skin and one of the highest concentrations of sensory neurons in his body.

30 The longer his ring finger is, the higher the chance he's the competitive, risk-taking type.

31 Is his index finger shorter than his ring finger? He's likely to have a bigger penis.

32 Check out the lines on a guy's palms. The straighter they are, the more laid-back and logical he is. If they curve, he's more expressive and an emotional thinker.

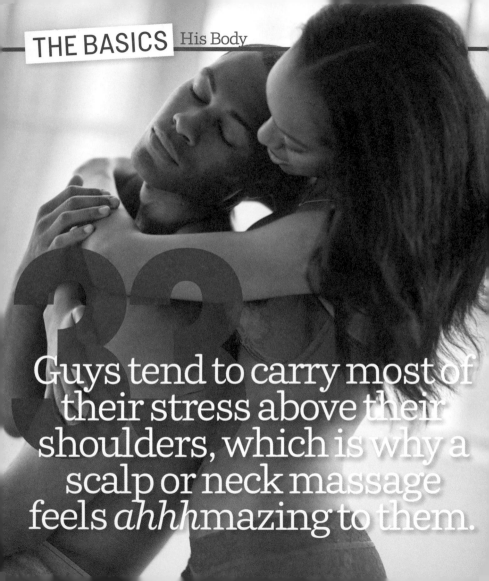

38

Guys tend to carry most of their stress above their shoulders, which is why a scalp or neck massage feels *ahhh*mazing to them.

34 Men have about 10 to 100 times more testosterone than women.

35 Guys' bodies are more efficient at sweating than women's, probably because all that extra testosterone improves their ability to perspire more effectively.

36 One scientific study found that 45 percent of men wish their penis was larger.

37 A guy's package stops growing sometime between ages 17 and 20.

38 Men who smoke are twice as likely to go bald.

39 The smallest penis recorded for a guy is five-eighths of an inch.

40 The average penis is about 5 inches long when erect.

1   2   3   4   5

41 Only 15 percent of men are longer than 7 inches, and just 3 percent surpass 8 inches.

42 The average man gets 11 erections a day.

43 If he gets an erection in public, he will usually attempt a technique called the waistline tuck: Watch for a hand-in-pocket adjustment that tucks his package under the waistband of his underwear.

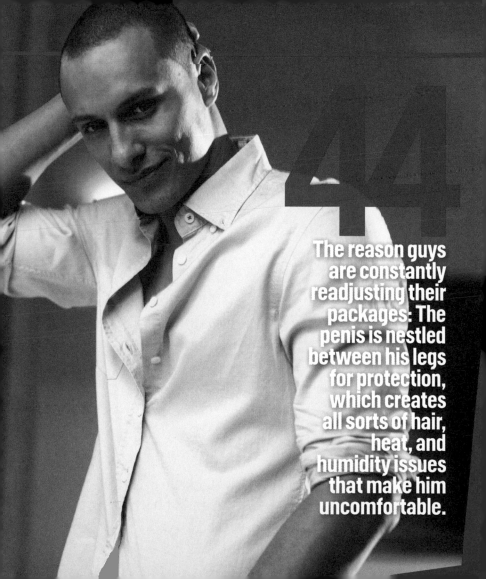

44

The reason guys are constantly readjusting their packages: The penis is nestled between his legs for protection, which creates all sorts of hair, heat, and humidity issues that make him uncomfortable.

His testicles should be about the size of walnuts in the shells, otherwise it could be a sign of low testosterone.

46

Some men's penises are curved—the most common direction is up or to the side.

47 For every 35 pounds an overweight man loses, his penis will appear to grow about 1 inch.

48 The average erect penis diameter is 1½ inches (and the average vagina is 1⅓ inches in diameter).

49 The penis has about 4,000 nerve endings (FYI: the clitoris has up to twice as many—about 6,000 to 8,000 nerve endings).

50 The average testicle is about 2 inches long and 1 inch wide.

51 And they should be the same size too, although it's common (and totally okay) for one of them to hang slightly lower than the other.

52 If a dude's anogenital distance (the length between his anus and the back of his testicles) is at least 2 inches long, he's seven times more likely to have what it takes to put a bun in your oven.

53

Take note of his ejaculate as well— if it's watery instead of thick, he likely has a low sperm count.

54

Worldwide, only 30 percent of men are circumcised.

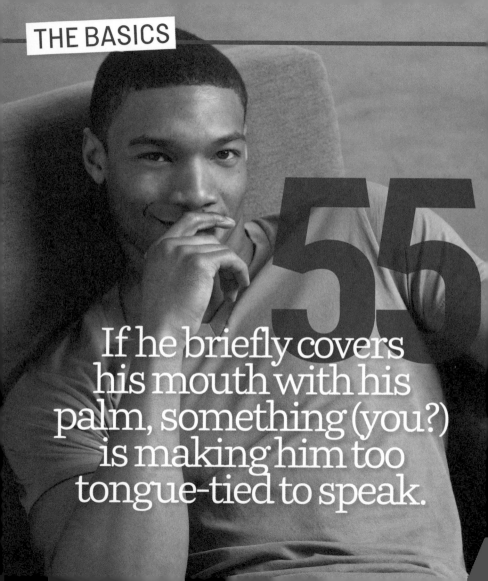

55

If he briefly covers his mouth with his palm, something (you?) is making him too tongue-tied to speak.

Body Language

56 Take note when he gestures with his palms up: It's a sign he's feeling comfortable and open. Palms down or in his pockets? He's nervous and closed off.

57 He'll blink extra long when he's lying. He literally cannot look you in the eye when he's fudging the truth.

58 If he hooks an arm around your waist and pulls you close, so that you form the letter T with his body, then he's proud to show you off and views you as his prize.

59

Notice a dude standing with his back or side to the bar? He's open to meeting new people, so chat him up.

60 When he pulls at his collar or scratches his neck, he's anxious or stressed.

61 If a guy waves good-bye while facing you straight on, then he's confident, strong, and genuine. By directing his body toward you (as opposed to turning his back), he's showing you he has nothing to hide.

62 Does he have a narrow stance? He's feeling vulnerable. A wide stance? He's saying that he can't be pushed around.

63

A guy will unknowingly give you the bird—think scratching his face with his middle finger—when he's upset.

64

Take note when he hangs his thumbs in his front pockets. He's subconsciously trying to draw your attention to his package.

65 A man who gestures with his palms down (or rests his palms on a table) is trying to assert control.

66 Does he nod his head when saying hello instead of waving? He's guarded, since he's litcrally not putting himself out there.

67 Usually, a guy will stand about 2 feet away from whomever he's talking to. So if he stands any closer, he's trying to connect and create an intimate vibe.

68

If a man wraps his ankle around the leg of a chair, it tends to be a sign of restraint—it's like he's physically fighting to hold back from telling you the whole story.

69

If he smiles with his lips *and* his eyebrows, he's genuinely excited to be with you.

71 When a guy licks his lips right after making a statement, it's often a clue he's fibbing...and he's trying to wipe the guilty words off his mouth.

70 A right-handed guy will often glance down and to the right when he's feeling anything deeply, from love to anger (left-handed guys will typically glance down and to the left).

72 You know how you absentmindedly play with your hair when you're talking to a guy you think is attractive? Men do the same thing.

73 Watch out if he rubs his face or ears—it can indicate he's lying.

If he angles his feet toward you, it means he's interested—people subconsciously direct their toes at the person they're into.

75 But if his toes point in toward each other, he's feeling vulnerable and unsure of himself.

76 And when a guy momentarily goes up on his tiptoes while he's talking, he's feeling confident.

77 Whenever he unknowingly points his thumbs up, he's mentally giving you a good review. For example, he may fix his hair with his thumb sticking out or hold his beer bottle with his thumb up.

78 A man who gives you a bear hug is the alpha-male type who likes to take charge, since he's covering your body with his.

79 When a man bites his lips as he's talking to you, it's often a clue he's hot for you.

80 If he does the finger point when he says good-bye, it's an over-the-top move that indicates he (and his big ego) digs the spotlight.

81 When a guy thumps your upper back during an embrace, it's a platonic gesture, so he's probably not that into you (sorry).

82 See a man tilt his head to the side when you're chatting? It's a primal come-hither move that he doesn't even realize he's doing.

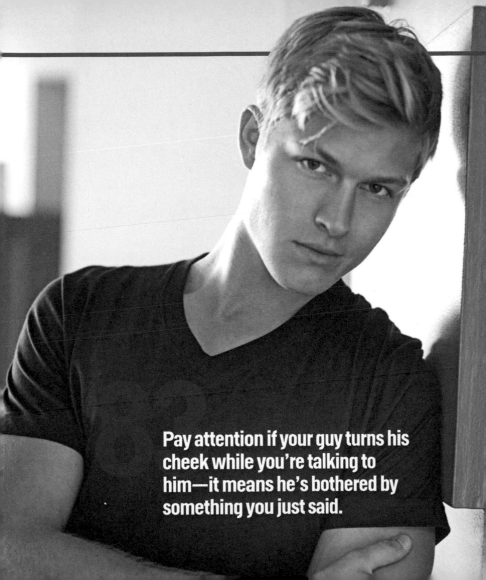

Pay attention if your guy turns his cheek while you're talking to him—it means he's bothered by something you just said.

84

A man who holds his drink in front of his chest is guarded—his beverage is like a wall he's putting up between you two. If he holds it down, though, he's feeling open.

85 Slouching doesn't necessarily mean he's bummed out—when a man is in protective mode, his shoulders will round like he's about to take you in his arms.

86 If you notice that his lips are tight and his jaw is slightly clenched, it's a signal that he's angry.

87 Men who give the half hug (a one-armed embrace) are more closed off and unsure of their feelings.

88 If he makes a steeple with his hands (fingertips to fingertips), he is cocky and isn't open to hearing your opinion. But if there's space between them, he's more willing to compromise.

89

When it comes to picking sides of the bed, men are often driven by instinct and sleep closest to the door to guard you.

Guys After Dark

90 Guys actually sleep better with their girlfriend or wife next to them (FYI: Women sleep worse).

91 When a man dreams about being in the spotlight as a hot celeb's main squeeze, he's likely hungry for extra attention from you.

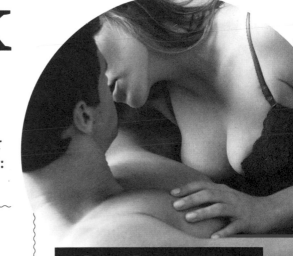

92 About 10 percent of men's dreams are sexual in nature.

93

If he dreams that he's desperately trying to fix a broken-down car, it typically means he fears he doesn't know how to please you in bed.

94 Men's top four nightmares, according to a study: He loses his job; he gets into a fight; his car crashes; and he's trapped in a scary place.

95 Dudes sometimes dream about having a threesome when something great happens to them—experts call it the celebration dream.

96 Did he have a naughty dream about his ex? It doesn't mean he's still sweating her—he's just longing for some aspect of a former relationship (like maybe he traveled a ton with his last GF, but you're more rooted).

97

Guys are twice as likely as women to sleep in the nude.

98 If a guy cuddles his pillow, it's a self-soothing move that suggests he's craving reassurance.

99 But if he clutches it, he's likely stressed—the grip is his body's way of releasing tension.

MATING CALL

When it comes to dating and relationships, men can be pretty cryptic. Luckily, you have us to translate. In this section, we'll delve into exactly what's going through his head, from the first time he sees a woman to when he's saying "I do" (and everything in between). While some facts will make you want to bitch-slap the nearest guy, others are seriously *aww*-worthy.

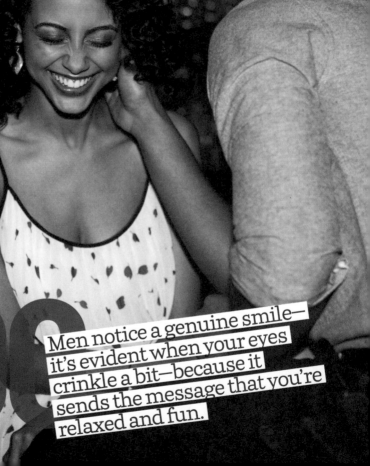

100

Men notice a genuine smile—it's evident when your eyes crinkle a bit—because it sends the message that you're relaxed and fun.

Attraction

101 Studies show that men are subconsciously drawn to women's voices that are in a slightly higher register, probably because it's a sign of youth.

102 Every now and then, you should skip wearing perfume when you're with him. Your musk conveys important info about your genetics, which appeals to his mating instincts.

103

When a guy is around a woman he's interested in, the erectile tissue in his nose will enlarge, causing it to itch.

104

Guys are actually attracted more to killer arms than legs, according to a scientific study.

105 Try this gaze that's proven to make you more alluring to men: Tilt your head down slightly, then look up at him. Scientists think it appeals to dudes' reproductive instincts, since your jaw appears smaller and your eyes seem bigger—two traits that suggest fertility.

106 He can't resist you when you bite your lip. Not only does it plump and redden your pout, but it also suggests you're struggling to figure something out, which sparks his curiosity.

107

There's a reason why he feels butterflies in his stomach when he's around a woman he has a thing for. The veins in his gut constrict, and blood is rerouted to his penis and surrounding muscles— that rapid outflow of blood triggers a fluttery sensation in his midsection.

108 If a guy has to compete for your attention, it raises his testosterone level, which gives his lust a boost.

109 A half-completed intimate gesture makes men want to finish it. So rest one of your hands halfway across a table, and it'll subconsciously make him want to grasp it (he probably won't, but he'll be charmed).

110 Men are wired to find your voice more seductive during that time of the month.

111

One study revealed that men rate women as sexier when they're wearing black.

112

The other color they can't resist? Red, according to a separate study.

113

He'll decide within seven seconds of looking at you if he's interested (to be fair, you're wired to make the same snap judgment).

114 They check out how thick and shiny your hair is. Lush locks are a primal signal that you're healthy (i.e., worth mating with).

115 When guys look at a woman's curves, the reward center in their mind lights up as though they were drinking alcohol or taking drugs.

116 Bare shoulders put one thought in a man's brain: boobs. So he can't help staring if you're wearing a strapless dress or sleeveless shirt.

117

Men are biologically attracted to women with full lips, since they're linked to fertility. (Bonus tip: Swipe on a pale pink lipstick, since it reflects light and makes your mouth look plumper.)

118

Guys are usually drawn to women with the same level of body fat as them—a process researchers call assertive mating.

119 Hot women make men nervous, so they tend to release pent-up tension by fidgeting (look for things like picking at his nails, shredding his napkin, etc.).

120 Researchers have found that men are more intrigued by altruistic women.

121 Noticing your ass may cause him to fall on his. Researchers found that male skateboarders attempted more dangerous tricks when sexy women watched.

122 Guys are more attracted to women with dark limbal rings (the outer edge of your iris). Rim your inner lines with white eyeliner to create alluring contrast.

123 Men ranked photos of women whose skin tone was the same all over their bod as the most beautiful.

124 The combined scents of pumpkin and lavender boost his attraction to you...and blood flow to his package.

MATING CALL

125

Men will subconsciously pick up on your speech patterns and mimic how you talk to seem more likable.

First Dates

126 He'll also suddenly lower the tone of his voice around you, so it has a deeper, more masculine register.

127 How's this for fair: Guys think a man only has to be a 5 (on the hotness scale of 1 to 10) to date a bombshell 10 but say a woman has to be at least a 7 to snag a 10.

128

If he opts for a macho menu choice, like steak, he's trying to assert his manliness to impress you.

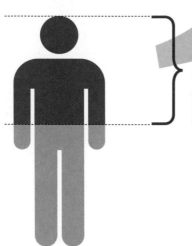

129 Forty-four percent of men say they wouldn't have sex on a first date.

130 If a guy chews loudly during dinner, it indicates that he's oblivious to the way other people react to his behavior, and that could also hold true away from the table.

131 When a man is into you, he'll concentrate so much brainpower on wowing you that he'll temporarily lose his short-term memory for basic stuff you tell him in conversation, like the name of your pet or the company you work for.

132

Doing something adventurous together on a date (like going to an amusement park or seeing a scary movie) increases the amount of dopamine in his brain, which automatically makes him feel more excited to be with you.

133

Watch out if he wolfs down his food—if he routinely finishes his meals long before you do, being in sync and savoring his time with you may not be priorities to him.

134

As he's talking, let your line of sight drop to his lips and linger there for three seconds. This appeals to his primal instincts, and although he won't realize why, he'll suddenly want to spend even more time with you.

135

Beware if he comes off as a little *too* mysterious—a man who doesn't open up about deeper topics like his family is avoiding bonding so he can keep things light (read: temporary).

Check out his wallet for more insight into his personality.

If it's messy, carrying all that junk shows he could be supportive... but that he also thrives on chaos.

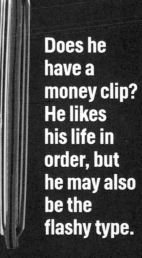

Does he have a money clip? He likes his life in order, but he may also be the flashy type.

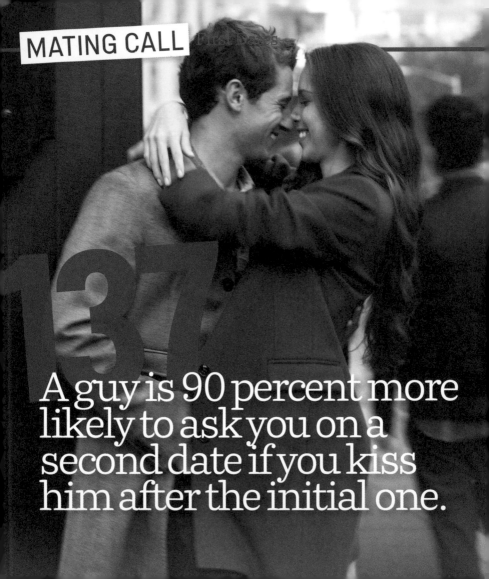

137

A guy is 90 percent more likely to ask you on a second date if you kiss him after the initial one.

138 If he's MIA after a date, use the rubber-band effect: pull away too, and his instinct to pursue you will likely kick in.

139 But if you *do* text him and don't get an enthusiastic response within 24 hours, delete his information.

140 Scientists found that guys are into women who say *I* often—meaning you should tell him personal stories and refer to yourself frequently throughout

141 *Thank You*

He wants you to offer to split the bill. A study found that when a man thinks he's being taken advantage of financially, the anger-management area of his brain lights up.

the date (just don't monopolize the conversation 100 percent).

142 Eighty-six percent of men stress after a date about whether you had a good time.

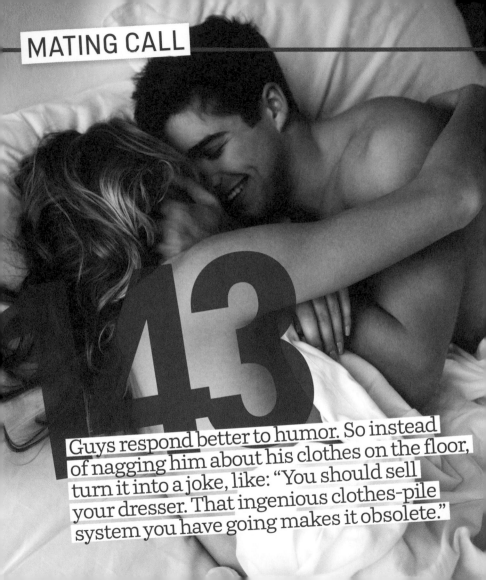

43

Guys respond better to humor. So instead of nagging him about his clothes on the floor, turn it into a joke, like: "You should sell your dresser. That ingenious clothes-pile system you have going makes it obsolete."

Communication

144 Occasionally, when you say one thing, he hears another. For example, when you tell him "I'm sure you would never do anything to hurt me emotionally," he hears "Wuss." Instead, say "I feel safe with you."

145 And when you tell him "I love you just the way you are," he hears "I love you in spite of your zillion flaws." A better option: "I love everything about you."

146 The best time to compliment him is in the morning—it will stick in his head all day long, magnifying its positive effect.

A guy who is lying will often use the number three in his stories, such as saying he had three drinks or went home at 3 a.m.

148 He'll also talk slowly to gauge if you're buying his BS.

149 One study found that the more a guy uses sarcasm with his girlfriend or wife, the less satisfied he is in the relationship and the more likely it is he'll break it off.

Men are more likely than women to interpret a friendly convo as sexual interest.

151 When you casually make statements like "I'll never..." or "I always...," men are hard-wired to take them literally.

152 When he clams up, it's usually for one of two reasons: Either he thinks you'll get upset if he says what's really on his mind or he's afraid of being emotional.

153 The worst times to initiate a serious talk with him on the weekend: Friday night after work (he's too tired), Saturday morning in bed (he's too relaxed), and when he's watching TV (his mind is elsewhere).

154 If you bring up an issue that he doesn't know how to fix (maybe something's off with his car), he'll often pretend it doesn't exist ("Nah, it's fine"), at least until he's had time to figure out what to do about it.

155

Men aren't as good at processing their emotions out loud, and that's especially true if it's something negative, like anxiety, fear, or guilt.

MATING CALL Communication

Testosterone Level
6 a.m.
7 a.m.
8 a.m.
9 a.m.
10 a.m.
11 a.m.
12 p.m.
1 p.m.
2 p.m.
3 p.m.
4 p.m.
5 p.m.
6 p.m.

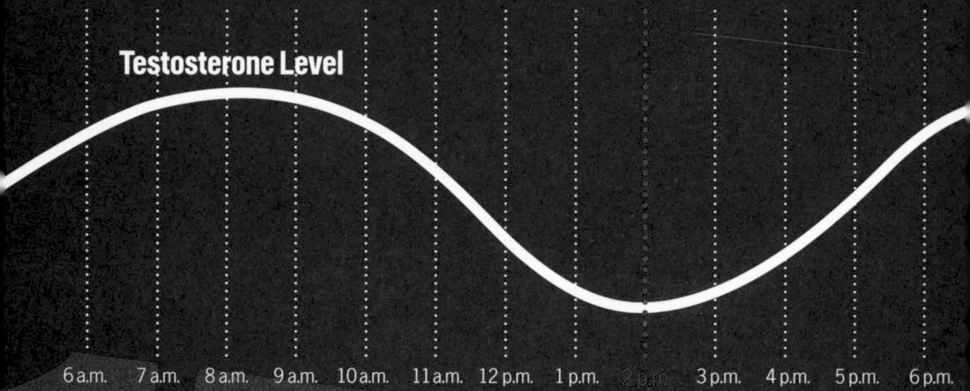

156

The best time to get a man to listen to you is at 2 p.m. His testosterone will be at a low in midafternoon, which means he'll be mellow and more likely to pay attention to whatever it is you have to say.

157 Asking him a question that begins with *Did you…*, *Will you…*, or *Are you…* usually results in one-word answers. Instead, start with *How* or *What*.

158 When you're just getting to know a guy, he'll prefer chatting about things (movies, sports) rather than people (his boss, his friends).

159

To men, words don't count as much as actions, which is why if they've done something wrong, they'd rather show you their remorse than say "I'm sorry."

160

The simple act of snuggling up to your guy will lower his blood pressure and make him feel more relaxed.

Love & Relationships

161 Men who are in an exclusive relationship still regularly check out other women around them, according to a scientific study. (Don't worry: The good ones are only looking.)

162 When a guy first falls in love, he resembles his partner hormonally—his testosterone level dips and hers rises.

163

One of the top things on his GF checklist, according to a Cosmo poll: listening. Men want a woman who shows enthusiasm about stuff that's important to him, from his job to his fantasy-football team.

164 Another thing on that list? You laughing often. Guys don't want you to be one of those overly giggly chicks, but they do want you to think they're funny—it makes them feel good and proves you're carefree.

165 When he's love-struck, his brain releases chemicals that make him feel gaga in one-fifth of a second.

166

Eighty-one percent of guys think a hookup can turn into a relationship.

167

Eighty-four percent of men say they prefer being attached to being single.

168 Guys flatline from the familiar, so variety is key. As a result, being spontaneous with him (like suggesting you two take a day trip to a cool nearby spot) doesn't just turn him on, it maintains his ability to be attracted to you.

169 On a scale of 1 to 7, with 7 being the most fun, men rate watching a romantic movie with their GF a 4.8.

170 When he's anxious, hold his hand. A study found that it'll decrease the amount of his stress hormones.

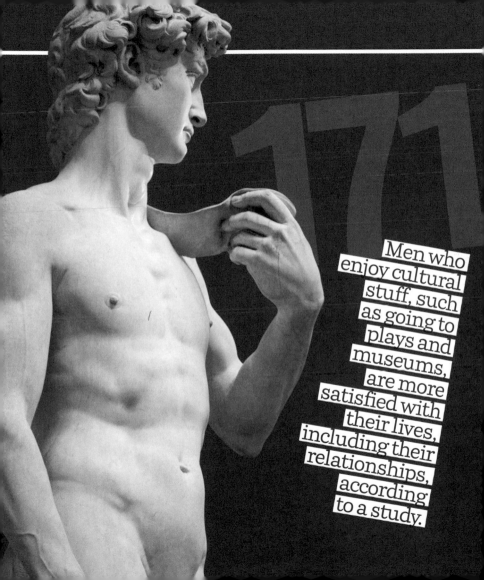

171

Men who enjoy cultural stuff, such as going to plays and museums, are more satisfied with their lives, including their relationships, according to a study.

172

If your guy isn't shy about crying in front of you, that's a sign that he's well balanced and an excellent communicator.

173 Seventy-eight percent of men wait until the day of or the day before a special event to buy a present.

174 Forty-seven percent of guys say they've fallen in love at first sight.

175 Men say that the top thing women don't understand about them is that they want to feel needed. If a woman is overly independent or ambivalent, he'll worry there isn't a place for him in her life.

176

Men are instinctively driven to be the protectors and providers, so doing stuff like carrying your heavy suitcase or opening that tight jar is how he expresses his love.

177 Once the relationship gets serious, guys worry the girl they're with will change. Their top three concerns: You won't want sex; you'll let yourself go; and you'll try to change him.

178 He judges whether he has relationship potential with a woman within three minutes of meeting her.

179 In a Cosmo poll, most guys said they needed one hour of solo time to cool off after a fight with their partner.

180 Unlike women, who are conditioned to take the pulse of a relationship now and then, men usually don't contemplate the state of their union until something's wrong. Translation: You'll (almost) always be the one to initiate a relationship talk.

181 Is your guy the strong, silent type? Men who are stoic will put you first (aw), but the drawback is he might have trouble opening up and letting down his guard.

182 If a man sees a future with you, he will make you feel like the two of you are a team—he'll start asking for your opinion on important decisions, and he'll say we more frequently in conversations.

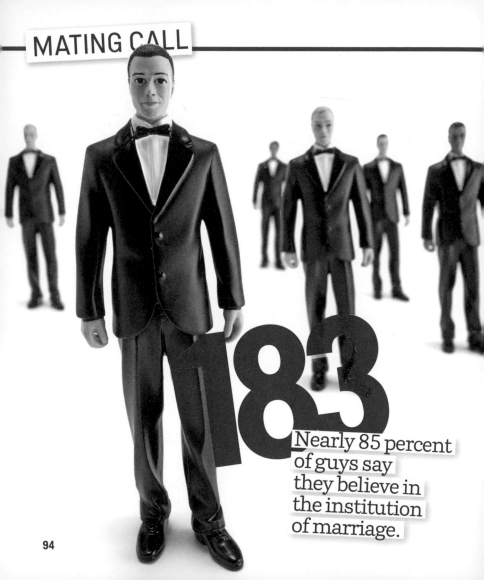

183

Nearly 85 percent of guys say they believe in the institution of marriage.

Marriage

184 Even if you've never discussed the M word, he might be feeling pressure to pop the question from other people, such as his married friends or even his boss and coworkers (research shows that employers subconsciously view married men as more dependable).

185 Approximately 1 in 3 guys will not pursue a relationship with a woman if they don't think she has wife potential.

186

Nearly half of men say they don't want to get married until they can afford their own home.

187

When evaluating qualities in a future wife, 90 percent of guys say they look for someone who will be a good mother.

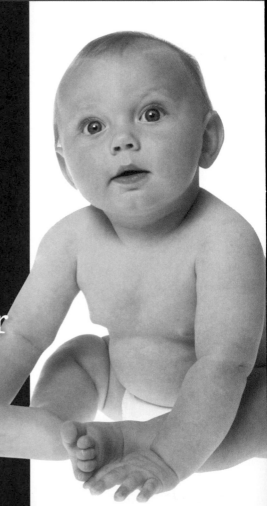

188

The timing has to be right for him. Relationship experts say that for most men, their decision to get married is 49 percent based on meeting the right person and 51 percent based on his readiness to commit.

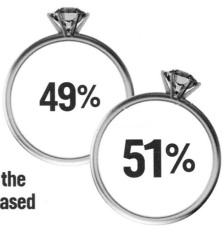

49%

51%

189 Three key give- aways that he's about to pop the question: He's extra helpful (he wants to prove he's domestic); he acts like you just started dating (his pro- posal buzz is bringing back those new-relationship butterflies); and he brags about stuff at work (he's hinting that he can provide for a future).

190 Eighteen percent of married men say their pets are better lis- teners than their wives are.

191

Sixty-five percent of guys have daydreamed at some point about their wedding day.

192 The top thing that makes a man decide she's The One? "She does something so amazing, I realize I want to be with her forever," according to a Cosmo poll.

193 While most women think moving in together is a step toward an engagement, a study found that guys view it as a chance to test-drive the relationship and to have more sex.

His shopping habits can reveal what kind of husband he'll be. Men who continue to search for options even after they've found the perfect item experience less intimacy and commitment and are less interested in getting hitched than guys who shop only until they've found something good enough for their needs.

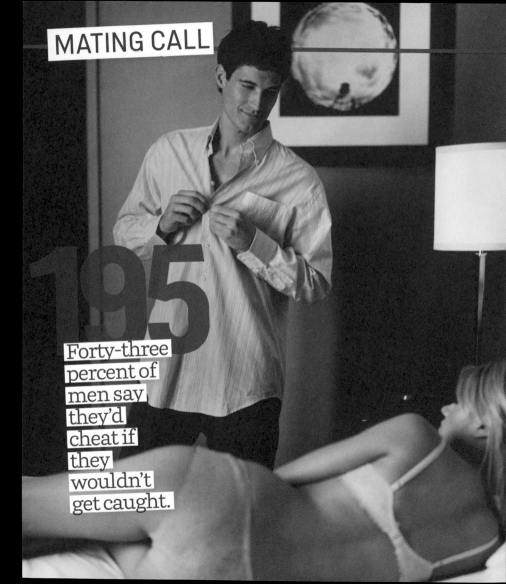

195

Forty-three percent of men say they'd cheat if they wouldn't get caught.

Cheating

196 If he gets along with your parents, he's less likely to stray.

197 Seventy-seven percent of men say they never talk about cheating—not even with a close friend.

198 A guy is five times more likely to cheat if he's dependent on his partner's income than if he earns the same salary as she does.

199

Scientists found that monogamous men have higher IQs than cheaters do. Experts think it's because smarter dudes have an easier time overcoming their primal drive to procreate.

200 Guys with manly features (like those to the right) are more likely to two-time. These traits signal that he has lots of testosterone, which scientists say amps up his desire to be with other women.

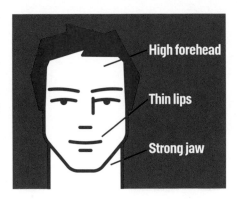

High forehead

Thin lips

Strong jaw

201 Guys often cheat down—meaning they have an affair with a woman who's less attractive/intelligent/fabulous than their partner—because those chicks will kiss their butts (figuratively or, hey, maybe literally), so they feel like less of a loser.

202 Another reason guys tend to cheat with a woman who's a major downgrade: 46 percent of men say that the mistress often agrees to try naughty things in the bedroom that he wouldn't dare ask his girlfriend or wife to do.

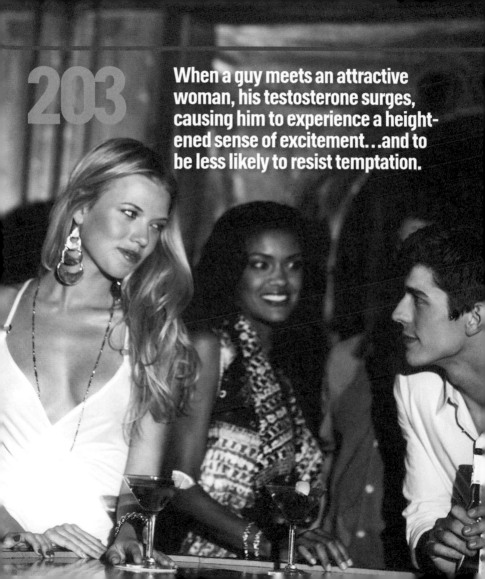

203

When a guy meets an attractive woman, his testosterone surges, causing him to experience a heightened sense of excitement...and to be less likely to resist temptation.

204

Three signs he's having
an affair: He spends
more time away from
home; he wants less
sex; and he avoids
your texts and calls.

206
Men are twice as likely as women to cheat more than once.

205 When an attached man is first crushing on another woman, the newness causes levels of the neurotransmitter dopamine to spike in his brain—it's like he's mentally addicted to her. As a result, he can't help but mention her frequently in convos.

207 But after a month or two, that new-crush buzz will wear off, and his guilt will set in. He'll stop dropping her name to avoid triggering suspicion.

208

If he was spoiled by his parents as a kid and continues to be as an adult (i.e., they baby him and help him out of financial jams), he's more likely to stray. That sense of entitlement makes him think he deserves to fulfill all his desires, no matter who he hurts.

209

Some men's tendency to cheat may be hardwired. Researchers found that men who inherit a certain gene are more likely to have an unstable relationship (which leads to infidelity).

210

Thirty-seven percent of guys say they could forgive a woman for straying.

211

Men thrust more quickly and deeply when having sex if they suspect their partner may be having an affair.

212 Guys are copycats:
A study shows
that if his best friend
has cheated on a partner,
the guy himself has too.

MATING CALL

213

When a guy wants to break up with you, he'll start to create space. A key sign: He texts less, and it takes him longer to respond to yours.

::: BlackBerry

oline (Mobile)
15, 9:50:09 AM

HEY! HAVEN'T HEARD
FROM YOU IN A WHILE....

Breakups & Exes

214 He also might bury himself at work. When he thinks it's over, he'll take on more to compensate; it gives his ego a boost, since he's upset that things with you are floundering.

215 Guys do much better after a split than they imagine they will, according to a scientific study.

216

Eighty percent of men think breakups should be done face-to-face.

217

One in three guys says he keeps mementos of ex-girlfriends.

218 Researchers found that when guys see those around them splitting from their significant others, it tends to encourage them to consider doing the same.

219 The top signs he isn't over his ex: (1) He compares you to her; (2) he flaunts your relationship early on; (3) you could pass as her twin.

220

Another tip-off he's pulling away: He stops inviting you to hang out with his friends. It's his way of letting his pals know that you're on the outs, and it also lets him bond more with them so they'll support him when the breakup backlash hits.

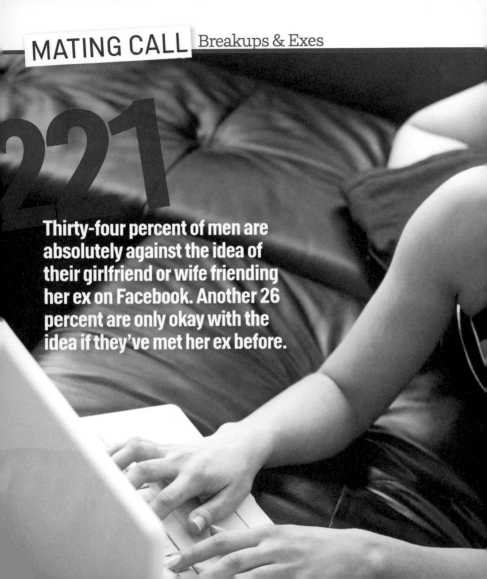

221

Thirty-four percent of men are absolutely against the idea of their girlfriend or wife friending her ex on Facebook. Another 26 percent are only okay with the idea if they've met her ex before.

222 When a guy dates a woman who could be his ex's body double, it's usually because he feels rejected by his former flame. He'll subconsciously choose to "win" a woman with a similar appearance as an ego boost.

223 There's a scientific reason why he has an easier time separating—he's less affected by oxytocin, a bonding chemical released by the body during relationships.

GETTING PHYSICAL

Ah, our favorite topic: sex. In the following pages, you'll find out all the titillating info you've always wanted to know about a man's lust life (but only Cosmo would tell you). The kisses he craves, how long he wants foreplay to last, the sex position that guys say is unforgettable— it's all right here. Read up and put your new sexy know-how to use tonight.

224

There's an undercover pleasure transmitter, the buccal nerve, surrounding the border of his mouth. He'll love it if you use the tip of your tongue to lightly trace the edge of his upper lip.

Kissing

227

225 If your guy's go-to kiss spot (other than your mouth) is your neck, he wants you to trust him, since that area has tons of sensitive nerve endings.

226 But if he pecks your cheek, he's feeling needy (it's easy access for when he needs reassurance). Your forehead? He wants you to feel protected.

A smooch on the right side of his body feels more pleasurable. That's because the left hemisphere of his brain, which is responsible for positive feelings, controls the right half of his body.

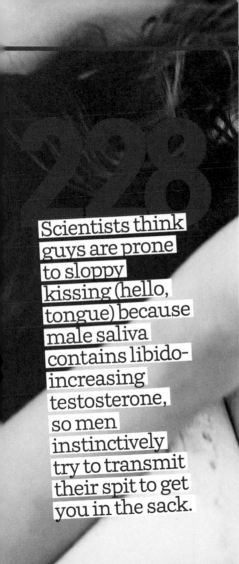

228 Scientists think guys are prone to sloppy kissing (hello, tongue) because male saliva contains libido-increasing testosterone, so men instinctively try to transmit their spit to get you in the sack.

229 Most guys associate lots of tongue with passion, so when he goes to town on you with his mouth, that's just his way of telling you he's smitten.

230 The amount of endorphins released in his body during a passionate kiss is equivalent to at least a minimal dose of morphine.

231 When he locks lips with you, he unconsciously matches his make-out technique with yours.

232

There's a reason why he loves it when you nibble on his ears: They are packed with nerve endings, have thinner skin, and contain no muscle—making them extra sensitive to touch.

233 During the excitement stage, his saliva changes, becoming thicker, and the flow decreases.

Give him a deep kiss, running your tongue along his teeth and the roof of his mouth to make him less parched.

234

Fifty-nine percent of men say they wouldn't pursue a relationship with a woman if their first kiss left something to be desired.

235

The no-fail move that gets guys ready for sex (according to them): a really long, steamy kiss.

Foreplay

236 Delaying gratification makes him fantasize about you more. When you tease him with sexy text messages or a peek of the hot bra you're wearing, his imagination runs wild.

237 Researchers found that guys' sexual fantasies are more often about their partner's pleasure than women's fantasies are.

238 Between 5 a.m. and 6 a.m. is when he has the highest level of testosterone in his body, making him extra horny.

239 It takes men and women about the same amount of time to get aroused physically, which is usually 11 to 12 minutes.

240 Turns out, men may not think about sex as often as we think they do. One study suggests that some guys actually contemplate fantasy football more.

241 The sexiest thing men say you can do when you give them a lap dance? Grind slowly against their body.

242 His lips will get plump and red when he's ready for action.

243 When he's excited down there, his penis will change colors. Arousal causes more blood to flow to his package, making it appear a bit darker.

244

When a man gets turned on during foreplay, his nose swells and his nostrils expand.

245

If a guy is seriously aroused, blood rushes to the surface of his skin, causing color to spread over his cheeks and chest.

246

The number one place
where men think about
sex is in the shower.

247 If a guy works out and lifts weights, he likely has a high libido, thanks to all that exercise-induced testosterone.

248 Because his inner thighs are right next to his groin, the extra blood flow to his genitals spills over into them, making them extremely sensitive.

249 Blue balls don't actually exist. Yes, prolonged erections can cause discomfort in the testicles, but he'd have to be constantly hard for several hours to be in pain (and in that case, it's likely a medical issue and he should see his doctor asap).

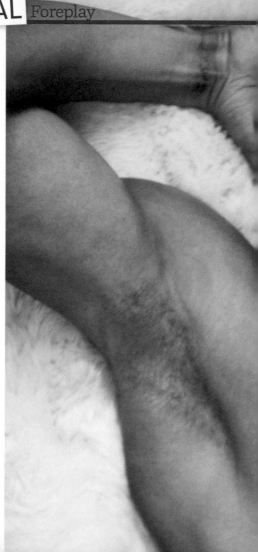

250 Your guy is more likely to disclose his fantasies to you if you promise him you won't laugh or be turned off. It also helps if you tell him a naughty desire of your own first.

251 When a man is really turned on, his toes will literally curl. Arousal triggers his muscles to involuntarily contract, which causes his feet, hands, and legs to clench.

252

That growers-versus-showers thing? It's a myth.
A man's package can look smaller or larger depending
on the amount of blood in his penis at that moment.

253

In the missionary position, a guy's penis forms the shape of a boomerang, curving up to hit the cervix, a trigger point for female climax.

Sex

254 His top three sex worries: he'll climax too soon; he won't be able to make you orgasm; and you'll get pregnant.

255 A man can actually get abrasions on his package from a particularly aggressive and intense sack session.

256 The average age when a guy loses his virginity in the United States is 16.9.

257
The most common male sex fantasy is a three-some with two women.

258 A study determined that men lose their desire if they're not mentally turned on. Keep him engaged with a position that packs an eye-popping X-rated view, like reverse-cowgirl.

259 Research confirms that bad boys get more action. Scientists found that dudes with personality traits like callousness, narcissism, and impulsiveness land more sexual partners over the short term than nice guys.

260 The sexiest sound you can make in bed, according to a Cosmo poll: a moan. Heavy breathing takes second place.

261 As a guy goes from his 20s to his 30s, his penis may not stand as high when erect. The good news: He'll get just as firm

262 Sixty-seven percent of men masturbate one to five times per week.

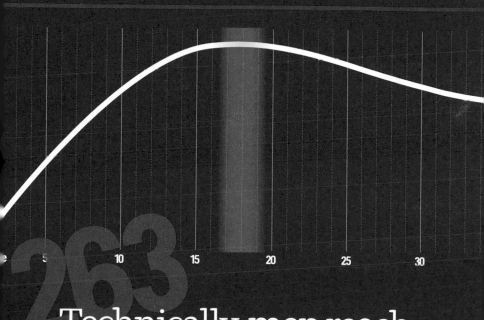

263

Technically, men reach
their sexual peak when
they're in their late teens,
since that's when they
get erect the quickest.

264

In a Cosmo
poll, men
voted girl-on-
top as their
favorite
position.

265

But doggie-style takes a very close second place.

266 When you touch the sides of his torso, it stimulates a powerful nerve that causes his pelvic-floor muscles to contract...and his penis to get even harder.

267 Initiate lazy-morning sex with him. Research shows that men who get it on in the a.m. are happier than those who don't.

268 Try wrapping a belt around the back of his thighs. This will push more blood into his penis, making his erection feel stronger.

269 When you're straddling him, stop so only his tip is inside you. Then squeeze your vagina like you're doing a Kegel—he'll love the intense pleasure.

270
Factors like stress, anxiety, and low self-esteem cause up to 20 percent of male erectile dysfunction.

271 Yes, a man can break his penis—if he thrusts really hard against his partner's pubic bone. You'll hear a popping sound, and his penis will bruise and swell.

272 When he's in missionary and about to finish, reach down and touch his perineum (the spot between his anus and his testicles) just like you would a button. You'll make his finale even more moanworthy.

273 His pecs can be as sensitive during the deed as your breasts.

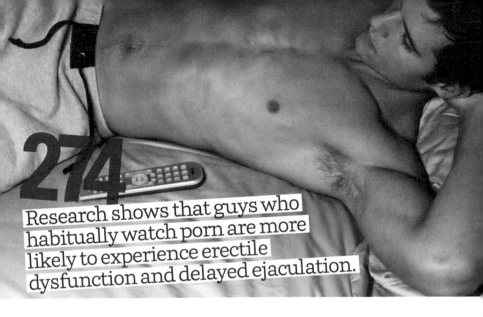

274 Research shows that guys who habitually watch porn are more likely to experience erectile dysfunction and delayed ejaculation.

275 The nerves along his spine connect directly to those in his penis. So during sex, glide your nails up and down his back or let your breasts graze against him—he'll get an intense rush down below.

276 Scientists found that men who do stuff around the house (wash the dishes, take out the trash) have more sex.

277 Looking at your face during the act makes men feel more emotionally connected to you.

278 The average number of partners for a heterosexual man is seven.

279 Most guys admitted in a Cosmo poll that they want sex (including foreplay) to last at least 45 minutes.

280 Seventy-one percent of men would rather have great sex occasionally than have not-so-hot sex all the time.

281 When you say his name while you're getting it on, the reward center in his brain lights up, instantly increasing his pleasure.

282

His number one role-play
fantasy, according to a
Cosmo poll: boss/secretary.

283

His orgasm lasts an average of 3 to 10 seconds.

His Climax

284 During his climax, he experiences about four to five contractions that occur at 0.8-second intervals, the first one being the most intense.

285 If a man ejaculates daily or several times a day, his semen will taste saltier.

286

Pre-O

Post-O

Levels of the hormone oxytocin in a guy's body skyrocket by 500 percent post-O, which deepens trust and makes him feel connected to his partner.

287 Right before he orgasms, his breathing will become fast and shallow.

288 Other signs he's about to blast off: His body stiffens; his penis subtly pulses; and his testicles lift slightly up toward his penis.

289 If he's close to climaxing but you're not, try this sneaky-yet-effective trick: Squeeze the head of his penis gently to decrease sensation for him.

290 The average speed of a man's ejaculate is 28 mph.

291
Seventy percent
of men believe their
partner never fakes it.

292

He shakes post-O because his body temperature rises during arousal and lowers after the event—the orgasmic shudder is a normal part of ejaculation.

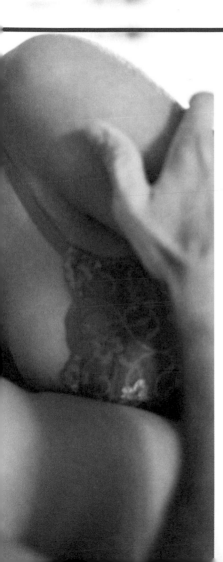

293 **Most men need just two minutes to go over the edge via intercourse.**

294 In the moments before a guy peaks, his brain basically shuts down as he's completely overcome by physical sensations.

295
Seventy-four percent of men say they climax every time (compared to 30 percent of women), according to a study.

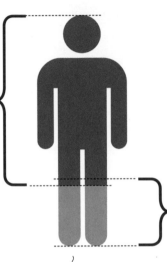

296
Another study reports that 28 percent of men say they've faked it.

297 Guys can have multiple orgasms, but they'll ejaculate only once.

298 Typically, though, most men need some kind of a break in between, usually about 15 to 30 minutes.

299 When a man spends time away from his girlfriend or wife, he ejaculates more sperm the next time he has sex with her.

300 Yoga can help guys who have premature-ejaculation problems extend their performance time.

301

Guys tend to want to sleep postsex because their bodies release a bunch of chemicals when they ejaculate, which chills them out.

302

You can tell a lot about a guy by his O face. If he cringes, he's been trying to stave off his orgasm…and now he's at his point of no return. If his eyes are squeezed shut, he's the type who really needs to concentrate on the physical sensations he's experiencing to get off.

303

Over the course of his life, a man will ejaculate nearly 16 quarts of semen.

304

Take note if his jaw is totally slack during climax. If it is, he's in the zone and 100 percent relaxed, whereas if his tongue is sticking out of his mouth, he may be feeling self-conscious about totally letting go in front of you.

OUTSIDE INFLUENCES

Just like you, guys have a lot on their minds these days—friends, work, what they look like, and even their Facebook profiles. Over the next few chapters, you'll learn a ton of surprising, secret info about each (like how much he *really* tells his friends after you hook up). We even analyze his manscaping habits and what his underwear (or lack of...) says about him. After all, it's our job to be thorough, isn't it?

305

His bromance has a positive effect on his relationship with his GF or wife because it allows him to better process his emotions and feel supported.

His Friends

306 Men are confused by how women can be insta-friends, since they're wired to be more guarded.

307 If your guy flirts a little with your friends, relax. It's usually because he's trying to prove his boyfriend-worthiness by charming your crew.

308 Men defend their friends (even if they do something douche-y, like cheat) because they've been socialized to have a brotherhood mentality. If he goes against that, it'd make him feel like less of a man.

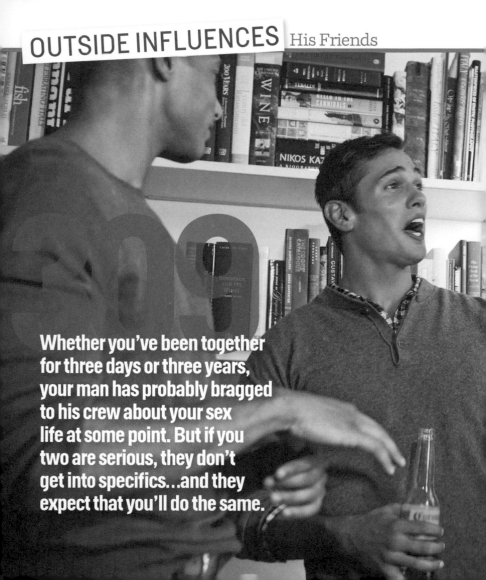

Whether you've been together for three days or three years, your man has probably bragged to his crew about your sex life at some point. But if you two are serious, they don't get into specifics…and they expect that you'll do the same.

He also tells his guys about that raging fight you had (he's trying to gauge if that kind of bickering is normal in a relationship) and that time you accidentally flashed his grandma (guys relate by sharing goofy stories… even if it's at your expense).

311 Forty-five percent of men say they flirt with other girls on guys' night.

312 When he makes fun of your friends, it's because he's used to that kind of joking around with his own buddies.

313

One of the best ways to win over a new guy is to secure the approval of his boys—since guys naturally have more of a pack mentality, getting the green light from them will make him more open to a future with you.

314

His friends can clue you in to key stuff about him. For example, if he's been close with the same guys since high school, he's loyal...but he may not be that great with change.

315 On the other hand, if he has friends from all areas of his life (work, the gym, college), then he's more open-minded and adapts to new situations easily.

316 When a man is in hot pursuit of a woman, sex trumps his friends, and he'll be available for the woman he wants to be with pretty much anytime she wants him. But once that love bond is formed, he'll feel the need to balance out his social life and reclaim time with the guys again.

317

Guys consider their own earning potential and career ambitions to be as important as their appearance is.

Work & Money

318 Male coworkers want you to get straight to the point when talking to them (i.e., start off by IDing the end result of a meeting instead of recapping who was there, what was said, etc.).

319 Thirty-five percent of guys ages 16 to 25 say they'd choose love over a career.

320 Men who pay with plastic tend to be spontaneous and crave status, according to experts. And if he uses cash, he's more likely to be self-sufficient and practical.

321

Men get their sense of identity from what they do for a living, so an unsatisfying gig can weigh heavily on his mood.

322 Keep this in mind: If a guy is reckless with his spending (e.g., he regularly maxes out his credit card with stuff he can't afford), he's more likely to be careless in other areas of his life, including his relationships with women.

323 When women display lots of emotion on the job, it confuses men. Since guys aren't hardwired to process feelings and logic at the same time, they don't get that women are able to do both simultaneously.

324

A study found that men who flash their cash (by taking you on extravagant dates, springing for VIP service, etc.) are more likely to only want a hookup buddy than guys who keep a tight(er) grip on their wallet.

325

A whopping 88 percent of men admit to fantasizing about one of their female coworkers.

326 Work stress can really zap his desire—it's the number one reason guys say they turn down sex.

IN BOX

327 Not sure if he has a shady credit history? Run this question by him: "A friend is in a lot of credit-card debt, and I'm not sure how to help. Any ideas?" If he brushes it off as a common mistake, he might have bad credit.

328 If you want to subtly scope out a guy's salary range, ask him, "What job do you want in five years?" If he talks about a corner office, he's likely on a high-earning track. If he talks about flexibility, he may value his personal life more than his paycheck.

38

If your fave tee shirt and jeans do more for him than a slinky black number, you're dating a laid-back guy who likes equally laid-back chicks. A man who's wowed by a woman dolled up in high-end designer duds places a high priority on prestige.

Fashion & Grooming

330 In one study, men who wore scented deodorant (as opposed to the unscented kind) acted more confident and secure.

331 More guys think it's hot to watch you put up your hair, exposing your neck, than watch you let it down so it falls over your shoulders.

332

Sixty-seven percent of men say they'd tell a girl if she had funky breath.

333 The lingerie guys say they can't resist: anything sheer.

334

The top three primping rituals he hates to see you do before bed: dotting zit cream on your face, applying (and smelling like) self-tanner, and greasing up with lots of lotion.

335 Thanks to the slinglike pouches and extra padding now built into some brands of men's boxers, guys are getting a lot more, uh, lift.

336 Sixty-four percent of men say you should save the ponytail for the gym.

337 Ninety-five percent of guys say they manscape, with 86 percent of them admitting to shaving or trimming at home (the rest either go to a pro at a salon or wax themselves).

338

Sixty percent say they trim down there because they like the look, not just because they think it'll please women.

339

He may say it doesn't bother him, but in a Cosmo poll, 65 percent of guys said they care if their GF has shin stubble.

340

Does he go commando? He is a free spirit and comfortable with his body.

341 But if he prefers tightie-whities, he's likely proud of his equipment and how he uses it. Men who like boxers or boxer briefs are less showy in bed, but they're more willing to keep the focus on you.

342 Fifty-nine percent of men think glasses on a girl are nerdy-hot.

344 However, ink on his lower back is especially personal, since that intimate area is rife with nerve endings.

343 Take note of the placement of his tattoo. If it's on his rib cage, it's something he wants to be reminded of often, since his ribs move every time he breathes.

345 And guys who have a tattoo on their thigh or calf are subconsciously flaunting their manliness, since they view their legs as a source of strength.

346

A guy who checks out his reflection in every store window he passes is obviously vain. But interestingly, it's also a sign of a dude who is intent on succeeding.

347

Sixty-one percent of male online daters lie about their weight.

Technology

348 If a guy is the type to never delete a single e-mail, he will probably be emotional and sentimental in his relationships.

349 Men are more likely to respond to online-dating messages if they're short—think 10 words, not 150.

350
Thirty-six percent of men say they're more attracted to a woman if she's using an iPad.

351 The area of the brain associated with reward and addiction is more active in men than women while playing video games. Well, duh. The cool part: Games that involve defending a place had the biggest effect because guys are instinctively territorial.

352 Seventy-one percent of men have read or would read their girlfriend's e-mail.

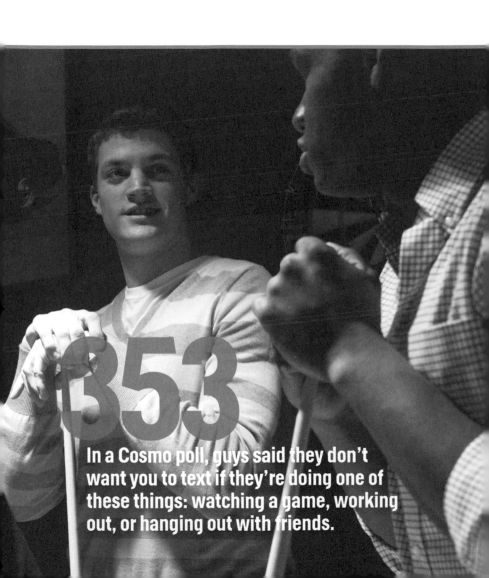

353

In a Cosmo poll, guys said they don't want you to text if they're doing one of these things: watching a game, working out, or hanging out with friends.

354

Guys are twice as likely to initiate contact with a woman if her profile pic reveals one of her interests (such as traveling or sports) instead of her assets.

355 Yes, he does judge your Facebook profile. Turn-ons: friends tagging you in pics (as long as they're not *too* boozy) and writing on your wall. Turn-offs: lots of status updates and a ton of applications.

356 The first thing he's checking out about your past on your Facebook timeline is what you used to look like.

357 And when it comes to your cover photo, guys say a pic of you and your friends is most likely to reel him in.

358

One in five men
plays video
games naked.

359

If he's giving a sweet smile in his profile pic, he's open and assured. If he looks like Mr. Serious instead, he's trying to broadcast masculinity.

360 And if he's making a goofy face in his photo, he's the fun-loving life of the party...but don't be surprised if he always has to be the center of attention.

361 The more frequently a guy checks out your FB profile, the more likely it is that he's the jealous type.

362

His DVR reveals clues about his personality. Does he have a ton of comedies? He relies on humor to defuse stressful situations but may have a hard time opening up for a serious convo. Lots of crime dramas? He's analytical and thoughtful.

CRACKING HIS CODE

Consider this section your cheat sheet to all things male. We have a dude dictionary of common phrases (turn to page 190 to find out what it means when he says "You're being such a girl") plus tons of tips straight from men's mouths—including your most burning guy-related questions, all answered in 20 words or less.

CRACKING HIS CODE

363

HE SAYS "I'm pretty much single."
HE MEANS "I have a girlfriend, but you're hot."

Guy Speak

	HE SAYS	**HE MEANS**
364	"We should hang out sometime."	**"I'm afraid you'll say no if I ask you out."**
365	"You're such a great friend."	**"I never want to date you."**
366	"How long was your last relationship?"	**"Are you looking for a fling or for something long term?"**
367	"Let's hang at my place tonight."	**"I'm hoping to get lucky with you tonight."**

CRACKING HIS CODE Guy Speak

	HE SAYS	HE MEANS
368	"My buddies are difficult to get to know at first."	**"They're not sure if they like you yet."**
369	"I'm not good at relationships."	**"I don't think you're important enough for me to put in much effort."**
370	"Let's not rush into things."	**"I'm still deciding whether you're girlfriend material."**
371	"You are so mysterious."	**"I haven't been able to figure you out yet and am feeling a little insecure about where I stand with you."**

372

HE SAYS "I've never been with someone like you."

HE MEANS "How did I manage to land you?"

373

HE SAYS "She got all psycho after we split."

HE MEANS "I treated her badly, and she got upset."

	HE SAYS	HE MEANS
374	"He seems like a good friend of yours."	**"Was there ever a thing between you?"**
375	"I don't get why girls like him."	**"I'm feeling insecure, so say something reassuring to me."**
376	"Isn't that a little revealing for girls' night?"	**"I don't want guys hitting on you."**
377	"That's not what I meant."	**"That's totally what I meant, but now that I see you're mad, I wish I hadn't said it out loud."**

	HE SAYS	HE MEANS
378	"Why are you being so emotional?"	**"Why are you acting like a psycho?"**
379	"I didn't know you'd be so upset."	**"I figured you'd probably get upset, so I didn't tell you before I did it."**
380	"You're being such a girl."	**"I don't understand you at all."**
381	"It's fine."	**"It's actually not fine, but I'm in no mood to discuss it."**
382	"It's just a guy thing, so you wouldn't understand."	**"It's going to make you mad if I explain."**

383

HE SAYS "I thought I knew her."
HE MEANS "I was checking her out."

384

"We love being seduced, so do it more often. Always being the one to start things sexually puts more pressure on us than you know."

Guy Confessions

385 "Please don't ask us to help you pick out what to wear. The brown skirt, the blue skirt—they all look the same."

386 "Ask us to do something for you, and you'll remind us that we're men. On the other hand, tell us how to do something, and you'll remind us of our mother."

387 "In the beginning, we'll listen to stories about your college sorority and keep saying how cute your cat is, but after a while, we'll stop doing that because we didn't really like doing it in the first place."

388

"When it comes to his penis, remember three things: If it's small, say it's the perfect fit. If it's average, say it's huge. If it's huge, he already knows, but he still loves hearing you say it anyway."

389

"We think about you more than you realize. We just don't call you up or e-mail you every time you pop into our heads."

390

"We let our guy friends know that we're getting it regularly, but we don't let them in on any details if we really like the girl."

391

"Too many women can't admit when they're wrong, so letting us know when we're right will score you major points."

392

"If you want our attention all the time, then don't give us all of yours."

393

"We're going to get pissed if you make us late because you're primping. But if you come out of the bathroom looking fantastic, (nearly) all is forgiven."

394 "We're sensitive about our bodies, but we won't admit it. Point out our belly flab, and we'll blow it off in front of you—then privately check it out later."

395 "Until we have The Talk, you should assume that we're still working the room and fielding our options."

396 "Making us ask for directions is like us telling you to ask another woman for fashion advice."

"It's actually not okay to pee in front of us all the time. It's just a little too familiar, you know?"

398 "The fastest way to get us to do something that you want in bed is to tell us what it is and ask if we're up to the challenge."

399

"If you ask us to carry your purse all the time, we're going to resent it."

400 "Anything we do that impresses you with regard to dating, we probably learned from a girl that we went out with before you."

401 "When we bring up something sweet we did for an ex, it's our way of broadcasting to you that we're good boyfriend material."

402 "If we're not getting hard, then you're probably touching it a little bit too lightly. Use more pressure."

403 "You may have heard that you can tell if a guy is good in bed based on if he's a good dancer. It's not true. Most men are too self-conscious about their moves to really let loose on the dance floor."

404

"If you want us to dress cool, buy us something that's comfy and we'll wear it all the time."

405

"Whenever you get up from the table at a restaurant, we scan the room to see how many other guys check you out."

406 "If we tell you that your dress looks nice at the beginning of a date, we're being polite. If we do it during the date, it's an excuse to stare at your body."

407 "It's a good sign if we tease you. We only do that to people we really like."

408 "Our web history will tell you everything you need to know about our secret sexual preferences."

409 "Every guy has one chick song on his iPod that he listens to often, but he'll deny knowing how it got there if you point it out."

412 "When we propose something kinky in bed that you've already tried, humor us and say you've never done it before."

410 "We know that girls burp and fart and stuff. But hearing you do it is a million times grosser than when we do it in front of you—not fair, but true."

411 "Don't read into what we say. We don't choose our words as carefully as you do."

413 "Wanting you to dress up in a cheerleader outfit doesn't mean we're weird. We're just trying to have the kind of sex life we never had in high school."

414 "Do not give us details about your period unless you're late this month."

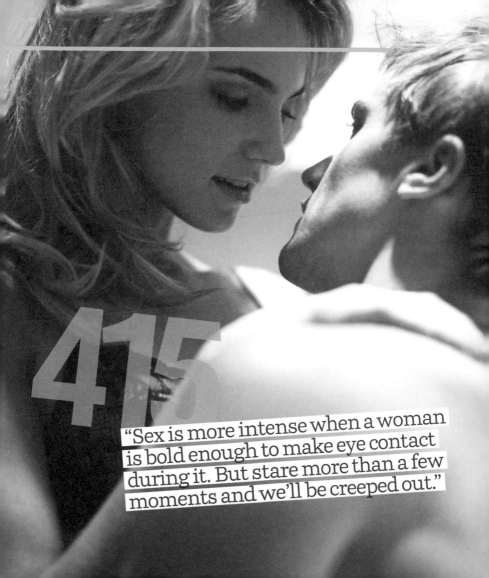

415

"Sex is more intense when a woman is bold enough to make eye contact during it. But stare more than a few moments and we'll be creeped out."

416

"If a friend of yours tells you she thinks your boyfriend is hot, don't tell him. Sure, the news will boost his ego, but it will also make him imagine having sex with her. And that would make you kinda angry, right?"

417 **"We like it when you wear skimpy clothes in front of our friends. Reveal enough to make them want you…but not so much that they assume they can have you."**

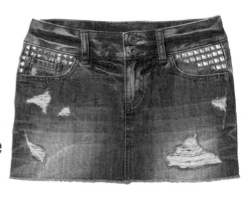

418 "It's exciting when you get angry at someone (just not at us). Seeing your aggressive side is like us showing you our sensitive side."

419 "Ask us how many women we've slept with, and we'll give you a low number if we like you and a high one if we're just after a short-term fling."

420 "Telling a guy he's nice isn't a compliment. The term has often been used as code for *boring* or *loser*, so we can't stand hearing it."

421

"If we ever walk away from you suddenly without any explanation, here's why: We had to let one rip or adjust our package."

422

"All guys masturbate, and most of us have been doing it every day or two since we first learned how to use the thing."

423

"We're so obsessed with your body that we're honestly blind to reading your body language in bed, so you have to speak up."

424

"If you hate a guy's mom, he'll think less of you, but if you always agree with what she says, he will also think less of you."

425

"Next time you insist on freshening up in the bathroom before sex, make it quick. The longer you spend behind that door, the more we wonder what nasty deed you're actually doing in there."

426 "If you really want us to watch more chick flicks, then don't tell your friends about the time we got misty at the end of one."

427 "Just because we occasionally look at other women in your presence doesn't mean we think they're hotter than you or that we love you less."

428 "We despise the word *cuddle*, but we have to admit, we love the feeling of our arms wrapped around you."

429 "Every so often, do something naughty during sex that you know will shock me."

430

When do guys view a relationship as serious? The moment they realize they're not sleeping with anyone else...and they're okay with it

Guys Answer

431 **Do men notice if you put on five or 10 pounds?**
Five, no. Ten, yes.

432 **Why doesn't my guy care if I drool over a hot celeb?**
Men are rational—he knows the chances you'll meet him are slim to none.

433 **Is it a bad sign if he doesn't insist on paying for the first date?**
Not necessarily; it shows he's secure enough in his manhood to split the bill.

434 **When my boyfriend invites me out with his friends, how do I know if he wants me to join or if he just doesn't want to hurt my feelings?**
If he uses qualifiers like "You can come if you want," he's just being nice.

435 **If I tell a guy "Nothing's wrong, I'm fine," does he actually believe me?**
Probably not. Men aren't always great at reading emotions, but when you say that, he knows it's a red flag.

CRACKING HIS CODE Guys Answer

436 **My husband doesn't have a lot of close friends anymore. Should I be worried?**
Yes. He'll start feeling isolated. Do something like joining a kickball league together to meet new people.

437

438 **What are men most insecure about in bed?**
That you might be faking your orgasm

439 **How can I get my boyfriend to warm up to my best male friend?**
Invite them to watch a sporting event together where they'll be rooting for the same team.

What screams high-maintenance to a guy when you first meet him?

When you put on makeup or check out your reflection in a window or mirror

440
How does he want me to apologize to him after I screw up?
Just make eye contact and say "I'm sorry"—most guys don't need more than that.

441
Do men with small penises actually realize they have small penises?
Yes; dudes look up things like average size.

442
So what could I say to make a less-endowed guy know that I'm genuinely okay with it?
Don't mention the size of his penis—just compliment the way he uses it during sex.

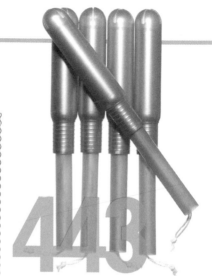

443

My boyfriend always calls me when he's at the store to ask if I need anything. At what point is it okay to request tampons?
If he's calling, you're close enough to ask. But do you really want to do that to him?

444 If a girl is crazy in bed, does that automatically make her not LTR material?
It can. So to be safe, get to girlfriend status before going completely rogue.

445 Why would he stay at home and manage his fantasy team instead of go on a date?
It's cheaper, he can do it in his boxers, and he doesn't have to talk to anyone.

446 After the first hookup, what does a dude tell his buddies about it?
If she's a fling, the entire play-by-play. If he's really into her, hardly anything.

447 What about after they've been dating a girl for awhile—what do guys tell their friends about sex then?
Subtle bragging at the most. Anything more and they worry they'll make their friends curious about being with her too.

448 How can I let a guy know that he uses too much gel?
Don't. Instead, rave about how his hair looks on the rare times he doesn't use it.

449 Do guys think it's funny if you burp in front of them...or just gross?
Most think it's just gross.

450

Why does he purposely let his hair grow out when I ask him to get a haircut? He's just being lazy, but he also thinks it's fun to annoy you.

451

Does it turn off guys if you make the first move?
It can—you'll feel like more of a catch to him if he actually has to catch you.

452 **Why can't guys ever tell when you get a haircut?**
He's focused on the big picture (how hot you are overall), not little details like your new style.

453 **Then why does he notice when my bra strap moves an inch to the left?**
That's the one area of your body he monitors 24/7.

454 **Why doesn't he defend me when one of his friends is rude to me?**
He'd rather risk a fight with you later in private than one with his buddy in public.

455 **Why does my man refuse to watch my television shows because they're "girlie," even though I sit through his favorites with him?**
Because he doesn't want even a small part of you to view him as being unmanly.

456

457 **At what point in a relationship do I have to tell a guy I've cheated in the past?**
It is never necessary and would just make him worry.

458 **My guy loves when I walk around in his shirt after sex. Why?**
It makes him feel like you're really his girl.

How come men never get distracted by things like their to-do list during sex?
They're hardwired to focus on one goal, so they can't think about chores while getting off.

PLEASE Take A Number

459

Why does my boyfriend never need a blanket at night when I'm completely freezing?
Although men and women have the same body temperature, women have a lower skin temp, which makes them feel colder.

460 **Why does he pretend** that nothing happened after he has a serious mood swing?
It's easier than explaining whatever he was really feeling at the time.

461 **I know guys think about other** women during sex. Who do they think about?
It could be anyone, but often it involves a celeb or replaying a past experience (sorry).

462 **If I don't get along with my** boyfriend's friends, does that mean he'll think our relationship won't last?
It's not a good sign.

463
What can I do to prompt him to make the first move?
Initiate subtle physical contact, like a fleeting arm touch or leg brush.

464 **I hate spending time with** my family, but he's close to his. Can I say no when he invites me to hang out with them?
No—you'd be rejecting something important to him. Plus, his family might actually be cool.

465 Why is it easier for guys to hook up without getting emotionally attached?
It's biological. His orgasm releases less of the bonding chemical oxytocin, which makes him less likely to feel a connection.

466

467 What do guys look for when they stalk your online-dating profile?
Signs that you're not crazy

468 My guy never takes me on dates anymore. How can I get him to start again?
Take him on one: Have him meet you somewhere romantic to get the ball rolling.

How can I get my husband to stop bringing his laptop into bed?

Say that a laptop-free bedroom is the only kind you'll have sex in.

469 He's usually outgoing, but with my work friends, he clams up. Why?

He either doesn't like your work friends or feels self-conscious around them.

470 How long should I expect a guy to stay and hang out after we hook up for the first time?

Not very long. Most guys won't stick around because they think that if they do, you'll think they're needy.

471 Why do men never seem to remember anniversaries or birthdays?

Since they think women overhype them, they protest by refusing to write the dates down...and then they forget them.

472 When a guy has had an orgasm (and his partner hasn't), why doesn't he offer to help her get there too?

He doesn't want to risk looking lame if he can't get her to finish. It's a pride thing.

473 Who do men turn to for advice and support when they're upset about something that's going on in their relationship?

No one, usually. Guys tend to internalize their feelings. But if they're really torn up, they'll ask a male friend.

474 What's a simple thing that I can say to nip his jealousy in the bud?

Tell him, "Let's get out of here. I'm tired of being around other guys."

475 Why can't men be more subtle about looking at boobs?

He'd rather sneak a good look and get caught staring than be subtle and barely see anything.

476 When I try a new move in bed, how can I tell if my guy likes it?

If he picks up the intensity, he's into it. If he slows it down, he's probably not.

477 One of my guy friends just moved in with his girl-friend but confessed to me he can't see himself actually marrying her. Why would a man do that?

Maybe she pressured him to move in; maybe it's convenient; or he could be downplaying it because he's into you.

478 My husband refuses to buy himself a new razor but loves it when I get one for him. Why won't he just replace it himself?

He was probably a mama's boy and secretly likes it when you take care of buying basics for him.

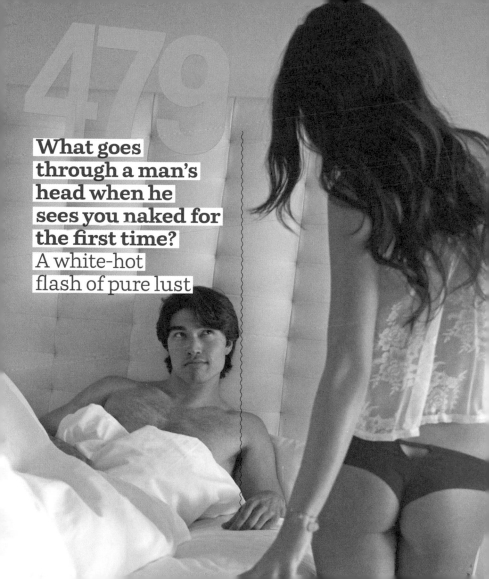

479

What goes through a man's head when he sees you naked for the first time?
A white-hot flash of pure lust

My man never wants to cuddle. Should I be worried?
No, it's normal—unless you've told him you want to and he still won't, which indicates he's insensitive to your needs.

481 **Why do guys seem to need nights alone so much more often than women do?**
Since they tend to be less commitment-oriented, it helps them feel like they're freer and not caged in.

482 **I gave my boyfriend a tee shirt, but then he got all weird about it. Why?**
A study shows that most guys feel indebted—not grateful—when you give them a gift.

483 **What should I say to my guy when his team loses?**
Anything but "Don't worry, it's just a game."

484 **How come men get so whiny about going to weddings, even if they always end up having fun at them?**
They don't want you to get any ideas and suddenly start pressuring them to propose.

485 **Why does my boyfriend freeze up whenever I try to have a serious talk with him?**
He assumes all serious conversations will lead to drama.

486 **How can I get a guy's attention at a bar without outright hitting on him?**
Hold his gaze a little longer than you would a stranger's. For dudes, that's a green light.

487

Why does he eat like an animal?
Guys are often just too busy enjoying their meal to think about maintaining their manners.

488 My boyfriend does romantic things, so why does he roll his eyes when he sees a guy do something similar in a chick flick?

Those moves are usually so over the top, it makes him feel like what he does isn't good enough.

489 Occasionally, my guy cries in front of me when he's really upset. How is he hoping I'll react?

By holding him and listening to him explain what's wrong

490 My boyfriend says I'm over-reacting when I tell him his female friend is into him. Can guys really not recognize shameless flirting?

He sees it but views it as a harmless ego boost. He'll downplay it to get you off his back.

491

492 Why do even non-players use cheesy pick-up lines on girls?

They work sometimes. And that way, if you turn them down, it's like you rejected the cheesy line...not him.

493 When he's down, what should I do?

Ask what's going on, but if he doesn't open up, drop it. He may just not want to talk.

How come he tells me he can't hang out then texts me all night?

He's not in the mood to spend the entire night together, but he still wants to keep tabs on you.

494 **How come men can't tell sexy clothes from the really slutty ones?**
They're too busy checking out a woman's boobs, butt, and legs to think about it.

495

496 **Why would he rather send me 25 texts about something than have a simple two-minute conversation?**
Because talking takes more effort. Don't let him get away with just texting. Next time, respond "Call me."

Why do guys turn into such babies when they get sick— even if they just have a cold?
Men will sometimes exaggerate their symptoms in order to get more sympathy from you.

497 **How come a guy feels the need to rush through foreplay when he's had sex with you tons of times?**
He doesn't need it to enjoy sex and hasn't figured out (or doesn't care) that you do.

498 **Why do guys always want their girlfriends to send naked pics to their cell phone? Isn't that what looking at online porn is for?**
Yeah, but when you're in the picture, it's like he's turned an innocent woman into his own private porn star.

499

Why do men hate throw pillows so freakin' much?
He doesn't like extra pillows because he's not sure what to do with them during a hookup.

500

What's the one thing men want to hear after sex?

"Wow"

CREDITS

Cover and Spine

Lynda Churilla

Contents

The Basics

His Brain

His Body

Body Language

Guys After Dark

Mating Call

Attraction

First Dates

Communication

Love & Relationships

Marriage

Cheating

Breakups & Exes

CREDITS

Cracking His Code

Guy Speak

Guy Confessions

Guys Answer

The End

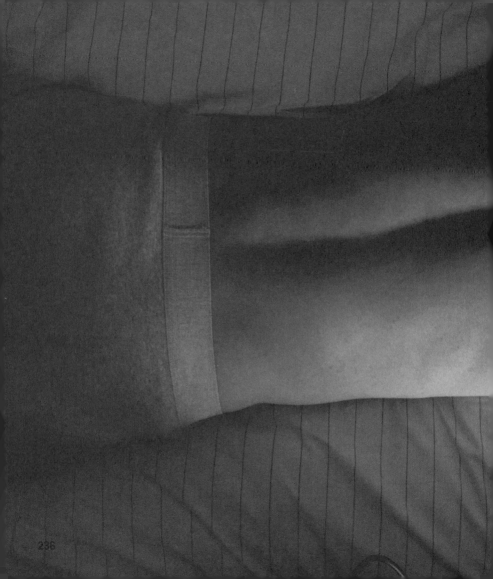

The End